Need It or Want It?

by John Serrano

You need some things to help you live.

Do you know what you need to live?

You need food. Food helps you live.

You need water. Water helps you live.

You need a home.

You need clothes.

Do you want things that you do not need?

This girl needs food.

Does she need this cupcake?

This boy needs water.

Does he need this milk shake?

This boy wants a new home.

This girl wants new clothes.

You want some things, but do you need them to live?